Gathoni Njenga

Author & Co-founder of
Corvus Web Services

A Beginner's Guide to Tribal Marketing©

A Beginner's Guide to Tribal Marketing©

Gathoni Njenga

OSTRICH^{TM}

Ostrich Publishers

Made in the U.S.A

www.ostrichpress.com

Ostrich Publishers

Charlotte, NC 28212

Copyright © 2020 by Gathoni Njenga

Ostrich Publishers is an ardent supporter and facilitator of creativity and the free flow of communication. We aim to inspire and help bring to the public quality literary works of independent Authors around the world. Thank you for buying an authorized edition of this book and complying with copyright laws by not reproducing, scanning or distributing any part of it in any form without permission. You are supporting writers and allowing Ostrich to have the resources to continue to publish books for everyone.

ISBN: 9781652418733

For more information about products and services or perhaps to make additional purchases, visit our official website at www.ostrichpress.com. We look forward to producing and /or publishing more books in the future. You can also visit Amazon.com or anywhere books are sold to purchase any of our other works.

Dedications

To the entrepreneurs and small business folk out there starting new companies and introducing innovative solutions to help solve the world's problems.

This is for you.

OSTRICH
PUBLISHERS

www.ostrichpress.com

"A handy guide to help you navigate the new realities of marketing. We are now more tribal than ever before"

A BEGINNER'S GUIDE TO

TRIBAL

MARKETING

GO BEYOND DEMOGRAPHICS AND START CONNECTING WITH NEW CUSTOMERS BASED ON THEIR COMMON INTERESTS

GATHONI NJENGA

For Frank, my partner, biggest fan, and the hardest working entrepreneur I know.

CONTENTS

A Beginner's Guide
to Tribal
Marketing©

Read First!

This book is meant to help you, the businessperson, the entrepreneur, go a bit further when it comes to how you sell yourself and your brand to newer audiences.

An attempt to introduce you to a newer more predictable way of audience discovery. Companies like *Netflix* and *Amazon* have been able to streamline their marketing efforts and increase their value as entities by using various tools to paint a more intimate picture of who their users are and how to create content, services and products for them.

This is what this book is about – reaching newer audiences, customers, clients, readers, donors...

Whatever you are into.

Welcome to the tribe...

I have always viewed the word as a dirty word. The word "Tribe". To me, this is a word that describes how folks behave when they suspend all concepts of independent thinking.

When folks start to act like a cult. The "follow the leader" no matter what mentality. Tribal thinking has caused more pain in the world than one can imagine.

In certain parts of Africa, The Middle East and around the world, tribal divisions are and have always been the reason, folks, oftentimes from the same family tree resort to acts of violence in an attempt to settle scores.

This is the reason (tribal behavior) we often fail to understand other people's differences in opinion, lifestyle, life choices, etc. The reason we cannot help but demonize those we consider "not one of us".

In my opinion, we are seldom at our best when we resort to this kind of primitive behavior.

That being said

In this book, I will focus on the more positive aspects of tribal behavior and how you, as a marketer and businessperson, can take advantage of some of the more predictable aspects of human behavior in the context of folks who share common interests and beliefs regardless of their varying demographics.

For us entrepreneurs, these folks are also a tribe, and selling to them based on what we know they like, dislike, and believe in is what we call *Tribal marketing*.

Marketing ourselves, our products, our services, and so on to folks based on what we know they are into.

Cards on the table

I think that the idea of marketing to tribes is nothing new. People do it all the time without actually thinking about it. Look, I will prove it to you. Let me ask you a question. During the holidays when you go shopping for close family and friends, do you just buy one item in bulk to wrap individually for the ones you love, or do you take the time to visit numerous online and offline shopping destination looking for and sometimes willing to pay top dollar to get just the perfect gift for each person on your list?

Now truth be told, if you chose option #1 then you suck. I just thought you should know that. But I am sure many of us take the time to get presents our folks will love. The kind of gifts they will cherish for many years to come.

This brings me to my main point. How do we know Uncle Benny will love this box set of the show 24, starring Kiefer Sutherland, all one thousand seasons? Because, he is a huge fan of the Kief, He loves conspiracy stuff – he is the kind of guy who watches *Ancient Aliens* on the history channel, and thinks *Alex Jones* is an investigative journalist and he may have mentioned that he only saw the last few seasons of the show before it went off the air.

See, you know that because you know your uncle, or you have at least had enough conversations with him to piece together what you think he might enjoy.

Christmas day finally rolls around, you give your uncle his gift and guess what? He loves it. Its his idea of "The perfect gift". Good Job you!

This is Tribal Marketing

This is essentially what Tribal Marketing is all about. You know what folks you know like because you know them.

The idea behind Tribal marketing is to get to know your audience. I mean really know them. Go beyond the run-of-the-mill crap and really get to know what makes them tick, what types of shows they like, dislike, and so on.

Look past your audience as it relates to whatever you are trying to sell them. Get to know them on an individual basis. Once you embark on this challenge and you start to make some progress, you will realize that, they, your prospective customer shares a lot in common with other folks.

Not just their age, race, income level, etc. Nope! Again, that stuff is the everyday stuff. I am talking about things that bind folks together. Folks that you would have never thought had anything in common.

Once you start to piece together a fine tapestry or map of what folks like and dislike and the other folks around the world who share similar interests and tastes, you will have started to uncover a tribe.

You will soon learn, with the help of various tools available these days, that they are even more likely to like a particular service, product, cause, etc.

Likes and shares

Speaking of tools... well, let me step back for a second and address a couple of things first.

In this book, I will often convey to you

the idea of leaving behind the older more demographics-based method of defining your audience. I will ask you to "dig deeper" into your methods through which you identify and communicate with your prospective customer.

I want to be clear that I am not suggesting that audience segmentation is obsolete, and that grouping your customers and prospects based on more common demographic characteristics is somehow a lost art.

No ma'am! I have written a few books on that very topic myself. I am a proud advocate of audience segmentation and the power it holds. I am merely asking that since social media, specifically Facebook has managed to develop tools to help marketers get a closer, more intimate picture of who their proposed audience is, I am merely asking that you build on the rich data demographics and segmentation provide and try to paint a fuller picture of who likes, buys, or is most likely to buy into your brand.

They are out there. We know this because they are constantly telling us what they Like and Dislike.

They share content they find interesting or utterly appalling. They make videos to constantly share their opinions with us. They support (publicly) folks they agree with and condemn, in similar fashion, the ones they don't. The tribe is in full force.

Death of Globalism: We Have all Gone Tribal

An end to the Obama-inspired Kumbaya days of yesteryear.

With the recent resounding victory in the UK general elections by Boris Johnson, "a huge, great stonking mandate" and the fact that Trump's popularity seems to keep soaring among Republicans - his base even as he stumbles his way through his first term, looking "very strongly" at toilets and sinks, something I try my best not to do, It is safe to say that we, humans are as tribal as we have ever been.

Those who identify as staunch supporters of 45 see him as a "great leader", while those who oppose his ascension to power see flaws in every move he makes. All while we all witness the same series of events.

We have all joined our respective tribes, taking extreme unwavering positions that we believe make us who we are: Conservatives, Liberals, Gun rights advocates, Woke, and so on.

I mean, millions of years of evolution have ensured that when all else fails, we retreat into our echo chambers only listening to the idiots who agree with us in the first place. We are all suffering from mild to severe cases of Confirmation bias as we render our opinions, views, and beliefs about a panoply of topics.

Thanks to the ubiquity of social media apps like Facebook, LinkedIn, Twitter and YouTube, folks can now only see and hear content that does nothing but reinforce our already existing often unsubstantiated, unresearched views.

It's not a Republican or Democrat thing, it's a people thing. We are all living in an era of self-aggrandizing.

A time when most people reject and view honest critical feedback as "hating" and gladly, willingly misconstrue difference in opinion as "fighting". The clap back era. And make no mistake about it, this type of behavior transcends age, race and all other traditional demographics.

We like what we like, hate (with unwavering fervor) who and what we hate, and we don't seem to care what others think about our public rants and often offensive outbursts.

We have all gone totally tribal

In some cases, we see this type of behavior bring folks who would otherwise not be seen together for the common good, and in other cases, this type of behavior leads to chaos, senseless conflict, and anarchy.

Social media was the main conduit via which young people across the Middle East mobilized to overthrow oppressive regimes during the Arab spring OF 2011. And even very recently during the Hong Kong Democracy protests. Again, folks with similar interests, views, and beliefs were able to quickly find one another to make their voice heard by the Chinese government. Tribes were able to communicate, organize and mobilize for change. The positive kind.

On the other hand, we also witnessed in horror as social media platforms like 4-chan and 8-

chan became the virtual tribal meeting spaces for folks who would seek to hurt others.

The modern-day Nazi and mass shooter, we know is more likely to have found a group of like-minded folks and become radicalized online.

Facebook is often the platform of choice when various hate groups and perpetrators of atrocities within our own communities decide to go out there, hurt others and broadcast their acts to their fans and followers. We know the New Zealand mosque shooter initially Live Streamed his reign of terror on Facebook.

Based on estimates by the Southern Poverty Law Center, the number of hate groups operating across America has risen to an all-time high of 1,020, mostly fueled by increased divisions among Americans, the mainstreaming of views that would have been considered repugnant only a decade ago, and the popularity of social media among many demographics.

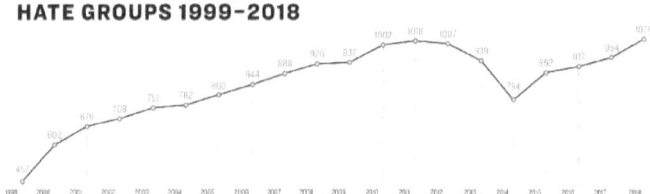

HATE GROUPS 1999-2018

Fear not

My goal in pointing out the good, the bad, and ugly sides of tribal behavior and efficiency that social media brings to the issue is not an attempt to scare the crap out of you or bring the mood down.

I am only trying to introduce the idea of the power folks have and the impact they can make once they are able to connect based on common beliefs, values, views, etc. This type of deep connection goes beyond basic demographics like age and gender. No, demographics, while still efficient, don't do as much to predict consumer behavior like tribes do.

Segmenting, as far as marketing goes, is powerful. Finding tribes, however, goes far beyond the tools and possibilities segmentation provides. Tribes are powerful and have been for thousands of years. Think about religion. There are, right now, billions of folks across the globe who share, if nothing else, a love for God, Jesus or Allah. This common love binds them, it serves as an accurate predictor of many of their most consequential daily practices.

Anyone or entity looking for ways to accurately foreshadow the behavior, or perhaps even inspire the actions and buying habits of any group of people need not ignore the shift to a more tribal global community.

Chapter One

This is Tribal Marketing

To engage a desired audience fully, we must learn to connect with them in ways that go beyond their proposed need or want for what we offer.

Marketing regardless of your line of business is about talking to folks who " speak your language". Audiences with who your message will resonate. Resonate enough to compel them to take whatever action results in you (and them) extracting a need-based or want-based value out of an action or transaction.

Such actions as simply exchanging their hard-earned money for your goods and/or services, donating to your cause, signing a petition for your grassroots organization, and many more. To engage a desired audience fully, we must learn to connect with them in ways that go beyond their proposed need or want for what we offer.

To the untrained business-type guy or gal, the challenge in marketing resides within the confines of trying to convince unsuspecting folks to buy into your brand message. This is a very common misconception. As a matter of fact, this is an issue I had to deal with time and time again when I launched my first company: An insurance agency.

I would watch as newer agents squandered their precious time chasing down folks who didn't see the need to protect themselves and their families, to try to convince them otherwise.

Needless to say, most of these agents soon tired of the whole thing and quit altogether. With a few I spoke, to no avail, of course, trying to let them understand what the true goal of prospecting and marketing was. And that is, among other things, the point of this chapter. I want you to understand why Tribes are more effective to market to.

What the point of marketing is, why simple demographics and segmentation just don't go far enough these days and to illustrate the power of tribal marketing in general.

Breaking it down

So, what is Tribal Marketing?

The term has been around for a few years now but only started catching on as time has passed and with the refining of the various processes through which businesses and marketers gather pertinent information about their customers.

The term generally refers to the ability for a brand to connect with audiences of varying backgrounds and demographics based solely on their shared interests, passions, beliefs, etc. One of the oldest but still very relevant forms of tribal connection, one that obviously transcends age, race, gender, even geography is religion.

There are about three major ones (religions) in the world, all passionate and growing in numbers. Aside from the spread of their beliefs, those who establish their organizations as ones that only exist to provide services and goods to these kinds of "tribes" flourish.

Tribal Markings

So how does one identify a Tribe?

How do you know what to look for when seeking out or looking to build a tribe? One that, in either case, you can sell your stuff to - Afterall isn't that what the whole point is?

So, some "tribes" are easy to find. They are obvious and make themselves known as soon as you see them. How do you know when you have spotted a motorcycle club on the highway or on some dusty country road? They all wear jackets with identical signage, right?

Yup, with some like-minded groups, you will not have any difficulty spotting their connection to one another. Some tribes, on the other hand, are a bit more difficult, at least at first sight to uncover.

There are, however, certain elements that will always serve as a guide to uncovering the shared values that make up a true tribe. One that is ready for connecting and conversations.

Characteristics of a tribe

Voluntary commitment

Membership to a true tribe, one that you will be able to really connect with, only requires that one joins of their own volition. All members of the tribe are typically folks who have decided to take time out of their busy lives to commit time and energy to be part of something. No one is forced, tricked or coerced to show up. Most members do more than just show up. They typically truly believe in whatever it is that connects them.

Vocal Advocates

Ever stumble upon an online forum or Facebook group dedicated to some specific idea, product, company or celebrity? Well, let me tell you this. The first thing you will notice about these types of groups is how vocal their members are.

I mean, the thing about the modern-day tribe is that with the help of various online tools and social media platforms, these guys and gals have many ways through which they routinely express themselves.

This is one of those things that when navigated properly and harnessed, as a business or brand can be of great service to you. The outspoken nature of members of each tribe will help spread the word about your products and services.

If you deliver on your brand promise, you will certainly have a bunch of advocates out there singing praises about your brand.

Like folks who love Lululemon. Surely the Vancouver, Canada-based women's apparel maker isn't the only brand out there making yoga pants. There are hundreds of brands that do what Lulu does, but those who wear those see-through yoga pants swear by them.

The company has managed to build a large network of users across the globe who are as passionate about the brand as they are about yoga and a healthy lifestyle. This group of dedicated advocates helps spread the word about the brand everywhere they go.

No Yes-men (women)

Tribes are democratic. Regardless of whether these like-minded folks gather around a product, cause or public figure, these are men and women who freely express their views and have an impact on how the overall group behaves.

This is especially true when looking at folks who organize based on their shared interests. Sure, a lot of times, "leaders" will emerge as is dictated and predicted by our very nature as humans, but these leaders are merely conduits through which the group communicates and interacts with other organizations.

The leader(s) serves only to take responsibility for certain administrative functions. Members express themselves and are heard whenever they feel things need to change or be altered in any way.

In fact, this is the very thing that sets the modern-day marketing tribe apart from what we all know tribes and tribal behavior to be.

Whether at group gatherings or via online platforms, folks that you identify as an ideal tribe for marketing will freely let their views be known even if it is in contrast with what other like-minded consumers believe.

Be prepared to have a process to receive feedback from members of your marketing tribe as this could be a great way to help improve your service or product.

Chapter Two

Harnessing the power of the tribe

Tapping into an engaged group of like-minded individuals who are passionate and dedicated to their beliefs can be a powerful tool in your marketing arsenal.

In order to realize the benefits of a successful interest-based marketing campaign, one that allows businesses such as yours to have a sizable audience with who your brand fully connects. One must first learn how to cultivate the power of the tribe.

You must take several steps to make sure that you and your organization are in a great position to recognize the potential increase to your bottom line and brand proliferation, curtsey of an engaged audience.

In today's fast-paced multi-dimensional digital ecosystem, it is easy for both tribes and brands to lose focus on what goals and objectives bind them. It is often the case when organizations fail to live up to their promise.

When this happens, said company or brand must invest heavily to try to restore their brand integrity and gain the lost trust with their audience and the public as a whole.

In this chapter, I will attempt to share some steps you, the entrepreneur can take to bolster your influence with your chosen tribes and to also to help you put yourself in the position to extract as much value as you can from your marketing efforts overall.

Community

Your customers are human, and like most humans, they love a sense of community. It's what we are. It is who we are as humans. This has been our earliest organizing principle. As a business owner looking to reach folks, you ought to keep this in mind.

Make building communities around your brand a centerpiece of your interest-driven marketing efforts.

Strive to provide the resources to allow your users/customers to form communities and to be able to fully connect and interact with one another.

Soul Cycle, the popular trendy health club

franchise, sort to carve out a niche in the fitness industry by building communities that love to exercise together.

Through this initiative, the company has been able to, over the last few years build a loyal following among its members.

People-powered

This should be your main focus: people! How you treat people, whether your customers or employees can make or break your marketing efforts and your business overall.

People are the most consequential part of everything you do in life and in business.

Most people in life want to be heard, seen, and appreciated. Sounds simple but in order to help drive profitability and overall growth, you will want to set up some kind of open system through which your customers and employees can provide feedback and voice any concerns or suggestions they may have.

Remember, when it comes to your target audience, these guys and gals share common interests views, passions, hobbies, etc. Creating new products or improving existing ones based on the recommendations of your customers will help you create a business the builds solutions perfect for your audience.

Customer experience

Cultivating a "customer first" culture will go a

long way to help build brand loyalty among your chosen marketing tribe(s).

Customer experience is essential to helping foster brand recognition and goodwill among your band of loyal customers and those you choose to target with your marketing efforts.

Great customer service, in today's modern hyper-interactive world, will involve you paying close attention to what customers say about your products, services and/or company and responding to their needs in real-time.

Netflix, the giant streaming service is great at responding to customer criticisms, requests, and overall viewing habits.

The company has been able to amass a global audience by being the go-to platform for customers of varying nationalities and viewing tastes.

The company's ability to cater their content to the needs of its loyal users is obviously a far cry from what audiences had come to expect from traditional television programming.

Townhall

Create a venue for your loyal customers to share their views and opinions about your brand. This is essential when you seek to target marketing tribes to help build your business. These types of customers are very passionate and vocal about the brands they shop or interact with.

Take advantage of this characteristic of your customer-type and allow them to share their experiences with your firm, as long as you ensure that most customer interactions with your company are positive ones.

The power of the customer voice is unrivaled when it comes to being the catalyst for attracting new customers. Customer reviews or word-of-mouth is truly second to none.

This is one of the greatest marketing tools you will ever have. Take the time and invest the resources to help your most loyal customers spread the word about your firm and its products.

Chapter Three
Going Beyond Demographics

Effective marketing today seeks to reach people not just based on their age, gender, and other demographics but based on their behavior, interests, etc.

As I mentioned earlier, businesses today, big and small must come up with new ways to reach new customers and form deeper connections with existing ones. This is the essence of building a brand. This is the whole point.

One must do so while maintaining profitability. This goal however lofty can be accomplished in many ways. Effective marketing today seeks to reach people not just based on their age, gender, and other demographics but based on their behavior, interests, etc.

For the purpose of this book, I shall focus on ways through which you can sustain profitability and growth through strategic marketing. Modern methods of marketing. Going beyond old ways of doing things and reaching a level of connectivity with your customers and users that allows you to help shape their view of your brand and more.

Reaching folks with your brand message. Letting them know that you've got what they need and giving them reasons to believe that your products and/or services will help solve some problem they have or provide some level of enjoyment.

We, as marketers, must constantly work to reach folks and tell a compelling story about our brand.

Compelling enough to make them want to whip that credit card out and spend their hard-earned money with us. Although successfully completing this task relies on many factors, there are ways through which you can streamline your entire sales and marketing process.

Tried and tested

In the old days, and by "old" I mean just a few years ago, before Facebook, LinkedIn, Insta, etc. Businesses and marketers alike were able to reach out to folks based on the little bit of information they could glean from public sources and surveys.

The way businesses would do it and by it, I mean customer segmentation and demographics, was that they (Brands) would conduct surveys with existing customers and general members of the community to try to determine which types of customers were more open to buying their products or using their services.

Companies would then use these

demographics to create segment models to help them determine how to improve their products and more importantly, where to deploy their marketing dollars. Over time, there were public sources available for smaller brands to be able to build these segments without incurring the high costs of conducting focus groups and customer surveys.

Companies like Experian and Sales Genie emerged to be two of the premier sources to go to when looking for demographic data on millions of Americans and folks around the world.

With segmentation, we, as entrepreneurs could make the decision to send out mailers, take out radio ads, conduct sales calls, etc. Based on what we know about a person's age, gender, ethnicity, location, etc. This was a tried and tested method of customer segmentation.

Segmentation and customer demographics..

Worked, or should I say has worked for quite some time now. I mean, don't get me wrong. Being able to determine some basic identifiable data about which folks are most likely to buy your stuff is still very helpful in building a robust marketing system. And even beyond that.

Consumer demographic data is great at helping you segment your users and customers into identifiable groups. Doing so can help you for one, create different versions of your products to reach out to the various segments of customers you may have and want to reach out to.

The Makeup industry, for example, went for years creating products that completely neglected the fact that women of color with dark tones were a big part of their customers. Supermodel Iman's cosmetic company was one of the first beauty lines to launch to specifically target women of color of all shades.

Having a clear picture, even at the most basic level of who your prospective customers are and knowing little details about your current ones will go a long way to help you build the kind of marketing and product development systems that will keep your brand front and center in the minds of the types of customers you target.

Then Social Media happened

The popularization of apps like Facebook and Instagram has helped provide marketers and entrepreneurs with a whole new world of data about consumers. With the help of platforms like LinkedIn, folks like you and I can now go beyond basic consumer demographics.

We can extract all kinds of consumer behavior, interests, affinity to brands and products, etc. From these social media apps. Facebook, in my opinion, is the premier platform to spend your marketing dollars with when looking to build or reach a tribe of potential customers based mostly on the types of behavior characteristics, they themselves have clearly stated they display.

Controversies aside, the social media giant has worked over the last ten or so years to build up a wealth of reliable data about their billions of global users. Data that you and I can tap into to help uncover various tribes of potential users and customers. Not to mention, help us understand our customer base on a much deeper level

Brands, in the 21st century, have quickly evolved to come to view their customers and users as not just names and numbers but as dynamic humans with depth and complexity. Today's customer will let you know when you have strayed from your mission as a company.

She will not hesitate to tell all your friends and family about your company. And thanks to these same platforms, she has the power and the voice to do so. As business folk, we must work hard to bring our customers and would-be customers in to join the process by which we create products and solutions and also help us shape the way we communicate with them and others like them.

Chapter Four

Walk a mile

Every successful relationship is built on three things: trust, reciprocity and clear communication.

That's it!

I mean, think about it. In any of your best

relationships, be it with your spouse, business partner, employer, church - yes, church! These three components exist, right? Especially in the relationships that stand the test of time.

Both parties get something of value out of the relationship, there is trust between all parties, trust that each can and will deliver on their promise and the ability for all parties to hear and be heard with next to zero misunderstandings. Any relationship regardless of how badly wanted will fizzle over time if all three are not present.

Your relationship with your customers, and by extension the general public is no different. Oftentimes, newer companies and some mature ones lose track of these truths.

So, if you are or hope to be in a long-lasting relationship with your customer base and each tribe of customers, you must work to establish the aforementioned elements.

In this chapter, we shall examine some of the

steps you must take within your marketing efforts and your general corporate culture to help build this coveted long-term relationship. The kind shared between brands like Starbucks and their customers all over the world. Or the kind of relentless passion folks have when it comes to their Apple products.

Listen with all your heart

Businesses today must look upon this element of relationship-building with the utmost seriousness. We must stand, ready to lend a sincere listening ear to our prospects and customers alike. Only then can we develop a full and rich picture of the diversity of needs and solutions required by our often-diverse groups of users, clients and/customers.

We must create various systems, whether online or offline to allow our customers to share valuable feedback with us. This kind of open-door policy is most evident with the way

Trader Joe's, #2 on Forbes' List of "Companies with the best customer service (2018)", treats and interacts with its customer base.

The Value health foods Grocer, over the last decade or so, has built various initiates around which customers, most of who live and work in communities where these eponymous stores are located, can actively participate with the development of new products, store design, inventory and so forth.

Employees at Chapel Hill Trader Joe's treat shoppers to holiday dance

What are they into?

Businesses and marketers today must recognize that their customers are dynamic individuals with varying needs, expectations and interests. During instances when we interact with our customers, whether during focus groups, online forums, or during customer support sessions. We must focus part of our efforts on getting to know our customers as segments and tribes and as individuals as much as we can.

We must extend ourselves to take notes on our customers' favorite pass times, ambitions, goals, etc. We will possess the resources and information we need to build a more intimate relationship with our communities of customers.

Large outfits like Amazon and Harris Teeter invest a great deal of time and money into getting to know their customers. With the help of AI and machine learning, the Seattle-based eCommerce giant, for instance, is able to deliver goods and services finely curated to pique the interest of each unique customer. Thereby making each shopping experience seamless and intuitive.

For customers, shopping is a breeze as the site serves up just what you need, even sometimes before you know you needed it. For the company, such predictive analytics has led to increased profits, cost reduction and brand penetration.

Harris Teeter, the Charlotte, NC-Based subsidiary of Ralphs, via various initiatives aimed at getting to know their customers, are able to tailor each store to the unique needs of those within each community who shop at their stores.

For some neighborhoods, their stores may have fully stocked wine bars, equipped with live music on the weekends. Others may have the added luxury of having a fully staffed bakery at their local Store, with catering and meal delivery services.

Harris Teeter, Pinehurst

How have others treated them in the past?

Whether we like to admit it or not, during courtship, when we are getting to know someone, the type of person we hope to date and more, this always comes up. Both parties at some point will express some pain points in our previous relationship.

This is a natural part of relationship-building. We tell the new guy or gal why perhaps we left the old one, or vice versa (although it is not often that we advertise why we were dumped). What we liked and dislikes about the ex.

Customers do the same all the time. Our prospective customers and our existing ones will not hesitate to express to us why they stopped using a particular product or service. Even more so these days as they (customers) now have a plethora of outlets to do so.

Aside from the general social media sounding boards, there are outlets like Yelp, TripAdvisor, and even sites like Capterra when it comes to software products. All these platforms are available to allow users and customers alike to share their thoughts and views on a range of products and services.

Let's face it. We are all living in the "how am I doing?" world now. As Comedian Bill Maher talked about in a recent "New Rules" segment. It is then our responsibility as business owners to listen carefully and use this information to build better products and ultimately better relationships with our tribe(s) of customers.

We must, as part of our on-boarding processes make every effort to inquire how our new customers found out about our offering, if they have used a similar product or service, and make every effort to find out what they disliked and liked about their previous experience. Gathering this information will help us curate every experience to meet the unique needs of our different groups of customers. More about tribe segmenting and curation later.

Announce your values

Go beyond your mission statement. Express, to your customers, prospective customers, and the community as a whole what you stand for. Let folks know what your values are as a company or organization.

Many surveys have shown that the modern-day customer or even employee wants to know where their company stands on a range of social issues. Younger audiences especially will go out of their way to spend money and/or work for companies that mirror or complement their values. Folks these days want brands to be part of the social dialog.

A recent poll by Sprout Social found that "two-thirds of consumers (66 percent) say it's important for brands to take public stands on social and political issues," while a 2017 Edelman survey agreed that "the majority of Millennials (60 percent) are belief-driven buyers."

Big multi-national brands, based on their research have found that when trying to reach a younger audience, they must strive hard to express their position on the social issues these audiences care about the most.

As was the case with Is Gillette's, controversial campaign calling out men to do more to fight back against toxic masculinity. Or Pepsi's Kendall Jenner, fight-the-power ad.

As a brand, you must take the opportunity to let your audience know what you are all about and where you stand on the topics of the day. Social media can serve as the ideal launchpad for your communication in this regard.

Kendall Jenner Pepsi Ad

Meet the family

My husband once told me that most of the brands he buys are relics from his childhood. He told me the reason he likes Calvin Klein's Eternity, although no one below the age of 60 even knows this fragrance exists is because this was his dad's favorite cologne growing up. He loves the smell of "Eternity" because it reminds him of his childhood.

The smell, he said, transports him back to his parents' house with his five other siblings playing pranks on each other and the countless movie nights they enjoyed as a family.

I am sure you have or know someone who feels loyalty to a brand or two because it is a favorite of a family member. As a business/brand you must adjust your marketing and brand outreach activities to cater to your tribe of customers and their family members as well.

Chapter Five

Follow the leader

Crown yourself the leader of the tribe. Show that you understand the needs of your audience and they will follow.

As I mentioned earlier, this book is meant to be a guide. A starting point to help you understand the need to uncover tribes of customers and perhaps build your own passionate groups of users.

Although, the "uncovering" part of this equation seems to be the technique du jour among many well-known brands. The truth is, it is far easier to find, cultivate and lead a passionate group of well-defined users within your own existing customer base than it is to define and build one.

Many top brands around the world typically look to their own customer base and with the help of various analytical tools and quick thinking, are able to segment their audience into various groups of tribes.

These brands will then figure out how to build marketing systems that speak directly and specifically to each group. The next step is then to go out and try to find new customers, fitting each into an already well-defined tribe.

There are, however, certain rules one must follow to allow for the investment and dedication of resources often required to define and build an entire array of messaging assets to help reach out to that group. For one, one must ensure that the economic payoff is worth the investment.

In other words, is that tribe or group of users or potential customers large enough to warrant the effort? Will you stand to gain, whether financially or otherwise by assigning an entire marketing campaign and all the resources required?

Most firms will also designate within their sales and marketing teams, folks that share common interests and views with the group of users being courted.

For example, if you decide to rollout a marketing campaign to try to market your new set of apps to millennials, you will not want to assign this task to your marketing guys who are middle-aged men and women.

Nope! You might want to assign this task to your younger group of marketers.

In this chapter, we shall take a close look at various techniques used by some top brands to help segment and define economically viable tribes of users within their own customer bases, how to go out and find others like them, and what the results have been.

The tribe you know

If you already have a sizeable customer base, you are in a great position to uncover real-life tribes of customers. The idea is to come up with a system that will allow you to continually identify and allocate certain markers that clearly define which group each customer belongs to.

The first logical step is to break your customer list down using some very basic demographics. Due to locational restrictions and costs associated with marketing in those areas, I will suggest that you do not use geographical location as one of these segmenting filters.

Not yet at least, unless you operate a brick-and-mortar business with no eCommerce lines of business. In other words, you can ignore the last suggestion if 100 percent of your customers come to your physical location.

Segmenting

The idea of segmenting your customers is a pretty straightforward one. Now, depending on what it is that your company makes, sells, provides, you will place a higher priority on some demographics over others.

For example, if your company sells cars, you will want to first divide your customer base by gender. This is simply because men and women buy cars for very different reasons and this would be the ideal place to start.

In this example, age will be the next logical filter. The next step will be to divide these guys up into whether there are children in the household or not and if the customers are single or married.

Now you know when you see someone driving a Minivan, regardless of age or gender, you know they have children, small children at that. Having kids or not plays a huge role in our choice of cars among many other products and services.

Now you will want to create some income levels and define various categories of cars that correspond with each income bracket. You will want to use some very general identifiers for these cars at this point. Perhaps instead of identifying these vehicles as sports, compact, etc. You will want to give them internal names that describe a stage in life rather than the type of car.

For example, you might notice that within your customer list, women under the age of 30, just moved to a new city, just got a new job making over 60k, unmarried with no kids tend to buy certain vehicles.

You can call this type the "Single Fresh starter(F) (mid-income)" Note that this is by no means a scientific process. This activity can be carried out with specificity that matches your current situation as long as it meets your needs.

The general idea here is to come up with a basic segmenting system that works for you. As you break your customers down some more, you will want to start to introduce some of the elements that will help determine which belong in which tribe of users.

Tribal lines

So, what is the difference between grouping customers by demographics and tribes? Well, the answer to that question is a complex one. I will say this though. Demographics simply identify what we are: Single, 30, female, etc.

Although effective, in today's vastly dynamic consumer landscape, we as business owners must go a bit further to stand out from the competition and connect wholeheartedly with our customers.

For that to happen we need to reach folks based on their interests, passions, political affiliations, stance on social issues, etc. As you build your business and grow your customer base, you will identify many elements that bind groups of customers within your customer base together.

You might even enhance your profit margins by creating new products and services to help meet the needs of these groups within groups. You will also undoubtedly uncover certain organizing elements unique to your business.

However, there are some well-known things that brands have used in the past to help group and reach their audiences. These elements evolve over time.

The main takeaway is for you to identify which issues of the day (if that is the route you choose to go) are important to your segments of customers and clearly communicate where you stand on those conversations as a brand.

Not personally, but as an organization. Although, it helps if you are a believer in the topics you choose to speak about. But remember, this is not about you. This is about what is important to your customers and larger target audience.

Examples:

Multi-cultural households

Goya Foods

Goya Foods wanted to promote inclusivity, largely focusing on helping Hispanic families striving to raise their children with a blend of both Hispanic and American culinary tastes. In a 2018 campaign "Growing Up with More Than One Flavor," the campaign's target audience was Hispanic parents who live in the U.S. and who had an interest in teaching their children about their cultural roots, and also encourage other people of non-Hispanic backgrounds to be more inclusive of their culinary choices.

Goya strove to position itself as an ally to families, providing the variety of ingredients that allow Hispanic families to explore both traditional and non-traditional recipes, thus enabling their children to grow up with more than one preferred "flavor" while also promoting the idea that cultural diversity and traditions are something to be proud of, not hide.

Notes:

It is fairly easy to identify the ethnic makeup of your customers and more importantly of any new customers you are looking to onboard. You can even take steps to add this question as an optional one in surveys and your initial setup of customers.

Let folks know that you are only asking this question in order to be able to provide services catered to their very own unique experiences.

Racial bias (Women of color)

Procter & Gamble

For the 10-year anniversary of P&G's "My Black is Beautiful" program, the brand wanted to expand its message beyond beauty and self-acceptance and address racial bias in America.

It created a video entitled "The Talk," about the conversation Black parents have with their children about prejudice, especially with self-esteem and appearance. The campaign increased the program's relevance among its target audience but delivered an inclusive message all consumers need to hear.

The "My Black is Beautiful" program consists of nearly three million women. Its primary target was African American mothers, and the program served as a way to encourage cross-

cultural conversations across communities.

The campaign spread awareness about beauty standards and how a lack of diversity can affect the ways people view themselves and others.

P&G campaigns to change definition of word 'black'

New moms and mothers to be

Wyeth Nutrition

To understand the parents the company serves, Wyeth Nutrition developed a data-driven strategy to and improve its message relevancy to parents of young children. The company, which develops premium-quality nutritional products scientifically designed to meet the needs of infants, young children, and pregnant and lactating mothers, wanted to find a way to identify different segments based on their unique digital habits. To do this, the company worked with Google to identify different groups and their needs.

After launching the data initiative in 2016, the brand successfully identified 198,000 pregnant moms and 272,000 moms. The use of data and segmentation also significantly improved the cost efficiency of Wyeth's media strategies: the cost per click lowered by over 30 percent, the cost per view of videos lowered by 50 percent, and the bounce rate on the brand's landing pages lowered by 20 percent. Best of all, Wyeth now has the capability to efficiently move consumers along a more personal consumer journey that meets their unique needs.

Single (busy) moms

Castorama

Creating a home that is not just a place to live, but a place that invites warmth, support, and comfort is necessary for all families. However, it's not an easy thing to do, especially when time and money are scarce.

For parents with young children who are also looking for ways to bond, French DIY *brand Castorama, known for decoration and home furnishings, created an activity that inspires home décor and storytelling.*

Castorama realized that bedtime is one of few times of day parents and children spend together. To help parents make the most of this time, Castorama's created "The Magic Wallpaper," an accessible, fun, and innovative way for parents to tell stories to children and was the first wallpaper to inspire innumerable adventures for kids ages 3 and up. For busy parents, single or not, bedtime can be one of the only times they get to spend with their kids; nearly 13 million French people were targeted, and the experience was available online before it became available in stores.

Conclusion

There are many ways you can reach existing and new customers. Ways that go far beyond the well-known basic demographics.

These are just a few examples inspired by the good folks at ana.net.

Once you embark on the journey to really analyze your database of existing customers, with an open creative mind, you will be able to identify various interest-based, passion-based, and lifestyle-centric ways that large groups of your existing customers are connected to one another.

You can then use this knowledge to build curated marketing campaigns and initiatives to appeal to these groups. Also, having this wealth of information will help you focus your overall business in a way that caters to your ideal customers.

Chapter Six

Outside extensions

Discover new marketable tribes outside of your customers base.

Mirroring your tribe(s)

Once you have identified various tribes within your customer base, how do you use this info to find more customers?

This is a very common query among entrepreneurs.

Sure, most folks get the idea of using these unique cohesive elements to group and appeal to existing customers in a much deeper fashion. We all get that for the most part but how do we 10x our captive audience?

In this chapter, I will focus on talking to you about a few tools and platforms to help you find external groups of potential customers similar to your newly identified tribes.

Getting down to the nitty gritty

In my humble opinion, there are three major tools that I have come across that make finding targeted audiences simple.

Sure, there are various tools such es Experian's audience segmenting tools that can help you delve into the most basic of demographic indicators when it comes to consumer audiences.

These tools like Salesfully, one of our apps, will help you create lists based on various segmenting filters. Ones that resemble those of your current user groups. The idea, in this case, is to find these audience groups, segment them and place them into your custom user groups, then deploy your custom marketing campaigns.

For example, in the case of the P&G's "Black is Beautiful" campaign. You would, if you were assigned the task of deploying marketing messages for this initiative, look for lists of customers who fall into the "women of color" segment. Simple enough. However, you would agree that simply choosing this single demographic approach would cast a very wide net, leading to higher marketing costs. Not to mention the potential of your messaging being taken the wrong way or ignored all together. A much better approach is to focus on audiences with who your very targeted message will truly resonate. Enough for them to take action.

What you will want to do is to find a way to focus on folks who through some indication of interest have signaled their "wokeness" and affinity to everything pro-black. You know, the kind of folks who wear Kenta outfits. These are the kind of folks with who you will get the most reaction. There are three tools I use to help create interest-based segments to market to.

Esri Zip code look up

I am not going to spend a whole lot of time on

this particular tool as it is merely meant to provide a basic starting point when assessing user demographics.

This tool is really useful when you are looking to launch tribal marketing campaigns that are location-based.

Perhaps you have a nutritional supplements shop and are looking to reach out to folks in the community. This tool will give you an idea of who lives in your community, what their ethnic makeup is, what their interests are and so forth.

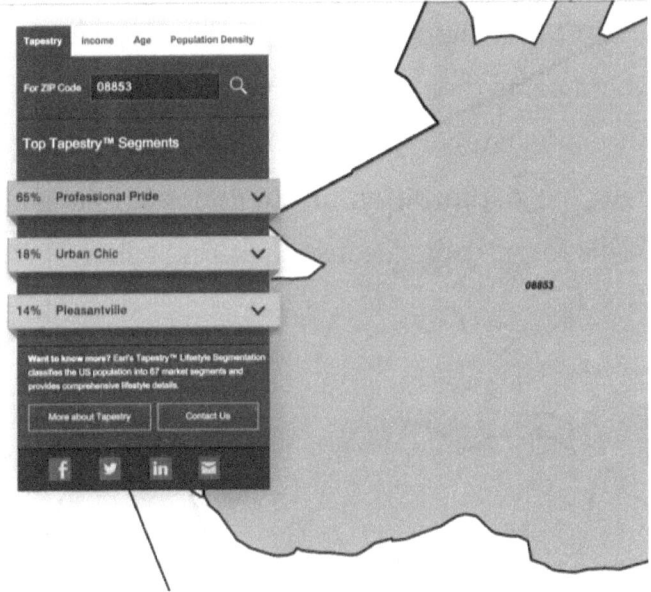

Facebook Ads (Create Audience)

If you use Facebook, then you are most likely familiar with their ad set up interface. The thing that makes Facebook's tools ideal when it comes to reaching out to folks based on their interests is that, in my opinion, the CA-based social media giant has invested billions of dollars to create a platform that allows folks all over the world to express their affinity for various causes, movies, games, TV shows, companies, etc.

This treasure trove of data is available when using their ad platform.

Of course, you will want to create a page for your organization and follow the following steps to suss out various marketing tribes.

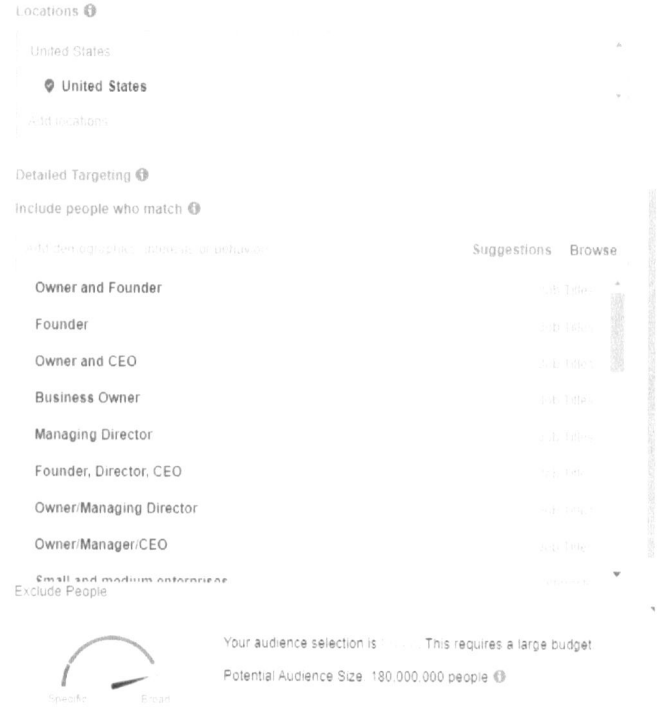

1. Create a new ad using your Facebook

account.

2. Create a new audience using one of the interest-based elements discovered during your assessment of your current customer base.

3. Use the "Suggestions" link to find more potential customers who's interests intersect with that of your individual customer tribes.

About the author

Gathoni is a serial entrepreneur and hobbyist. Over the last ten years, she, along with her husband and business partner, Frank have founded and run various businesses.

The couple started out by starting an

independent insurance agency. A business they still own and operate. Their agency opened its doors in 2011. The same year they met.

The company was initially started by Frank. Gathoni soon joined as a partner. They grew the company into a profitable venture and later started Corvus (www.corvus.website), a software business that was started as a way for them to build software solutions for their insurance business.

Soon, other businesses were subscribing to what has become numerous software applications.

The couple is currently investors and partners in various other business ventures. They spend most of their time in Charlotte, North Carolina, where they live. Gathoni is originally from Kenya, Africa where she was born and raised till she moved to Raleigh, North Carolina. Gathoni has always had an entrepreneurial spirit. Seeing her Grandfather build, along with her Grandmother, the family business.

She always wanted to start her own company, and soon did after college and a few years in the corporate world. Today, Gathoni spends her time running her business and writing business and sales books whenever she gets some free time.

She has, till date published over four business books.

All her books can be purchased at www.ostrichpress.com or on Amazon.com.

`

"A handy guide to help you navigate the new realities of marketing. We are now more tribal than ever before"

A BEGINNER'S GUIDE TO *TRIBAL* MARKETING

GO BEYOND DEMOGRAPHICS AND START CONNECTING WITH NEW CUSTOMERS BASED ON THEIR COMMON INTERESTS

GATHONI NJENGA

"A handy guide to help you navigate the new realities of marketing. We are now more tribal than ever before"

A BEGINNER'S GUIDE TO

TRIBAL

MARKETING

GO BEYOND DEMOGRAPHICS
AND START CONNECTING WITH
NEW CUSTOMERS BASED ON
THEIR COMMON INTERESTS

GATHONI NJENGA

Ostrich Publishers

Charlotte, NC 28212

ISBN: 9781652418733

For more information about products and services or perhaps to make additional purchases, visit our official website at www.ostrichpress.com. We look forward to producing and /or publishing more books in the future. You can also visit Amazon.com or anywhere books are sold to purchase any of our other works.

While the author has made every effort to provide accurate telephone numbers, internet addresses, and other contact information at the time of publication of this book, neither the publisher nor the author assumes any responsibility for errors or for changes that occur after publication. In addition, the author assumes no responsibility for the accuracy of any information presented here in this book.

A BEGINNER'S GUIDE TO *TRIBAL* *MARKETING*

GO BEYOND DEMOGRAPHICS AND START CONNECTING WITH NEW CUSTOMERS BASED ON THEIR COMMON INTERESTS

GATHONI NJENGA

TM

OSTRICH

Ostrich Publishers

Made in the U.S.A

www.ostrichpress.com